SGL Presents...

THE DEFINITIVE

HARRY POTTER

G·U·I·D·E B·O·O·K
SERIES
Book 4 - The Goblet of Fire

Book 4 Synopsis

We join the dark lord Voldemort and his follower Wormtail in Riddle House, plotting to abduct Harry Potter. Voldemort still suffers the effects of his last two meetings with Harry and is but a horrible skull on a useless body. Nevertheless, his reign of destruction has already begun. He has already interrogated and killed the dozy Ministry of Magic employee Bertha Jorkins. And he does not hesitate to murder the old gardener, Frank Bryce, who comes upon his hide-out in the old Riddle House.

Voldemort's attack on Bryce reverberates on Harry Potter's scar. The pain wakes Harry from his sleep two hundred miles away at the Dursleys', where he is once again spending his summer holidays. Harry is not having a very good summer, although he is grateful to have his books and school trunk with him—instead of locked away in the cupboard under the stairs. He is also grateful that his friends have sent him a stash of cakes and goodies so that he does not have to stick to the "diet" his overweight cousin Dudley is on. And his holidays take a marked turn for the better when the Weasleys invite him to the Quidditch World Cup.

The Weasleys come for Harry on a Sunday afternoon. They travel by floo powder and arrive in the Dursleys' blocked up, electric fireplace. A great fuss and commotion ensue before they leave with Harry and head home to The Burrow. That's because greedy Dudley makes the mistake of trying one of the twins' Ton-Tongue Toffees, with hilarious results.

The whole Weasley household is excited about the Quidditch World Cup, which one hundred thousand wizards from around the

world are expected to attend. Bill, Charlie and Percy Weasley apparate to the game, but the rest of the family uses a portkey on Stoatshead Hill. This particular portkey is an enchanted old boot which transports those touching it to the campground area near the World Cup site. Most of the tents in the campground show signs of their owners' efforts to make them as muggle-like as possible, in spite of features like chimneys and weather vanes. Some are obviously magical, with several storeys, turrets, gardens, and even live peacocks. The Weasley party puts up their tent by hand—the muggle way—and Harry is delighted to discover that its interior is a three-room apartment with a kitchen and bathroom.

The campsite is just across a wood from the quidditch pitch—an enormous, golden-walled field large enough to hold ten cathedrals. The stairs are carpeted in purple and every inch is enchanted with anti-muggle spells. The Weasleys have prime seats in the top box, and even having to sit with the Malfoys doesn't dampen anyone's good spirits. Fred and George Weasley bet all their money on the Irish team to win and on Bulgaria's star player, Viktor Krum, to get the golden snitch. After an exciting, rough and tumble game, Ireland takes the cup with a score of one hundred and seventy points. Bulgaria has one hundred and sixty, all but ten points of which are earned when seeker Krum catches the snitch in a dazzling display of flying.

The celebrations at the wizard campsites last through the night, until the revellers are interrupted by a crowd of hooded wizards who are amusing themselves by levitating the poor, terrified Roberts family—the muggle managers of the campground. The older

Weasleys go off to help their ministry colleagues get the situation under control, while Harry, Ron and Hermione take shelter in the woods. The three friends hear stumbling footsteps and an eerie voice shouting the word "*morsmordre!*" A huge dark mark appears in the sky and chaos erupts. Winky the house-elf is discovered with Harry's wand, which is shown to have conjured the mark. The Ministry of Magic is soon taken to task for lax security, and a bad situation is made worse by *Daily Prophet* reporter Rita Skeeter's highly biased reporting. The holidays are definitely over.

Ron, Hermione, and Harry board the Hogwarts Express for the start of their fourth year at wizarding school. Following the annual sorting hat ceremony, they learn that Mad-Eye Moody is to instruct Defense Against the Dark Arts. They also learn that the annual inter-house Quidditch Cup matches have been cancelled to accommodate the reinstated Triwizard Tournament. The three large European wizarding schools—Beauxbatons, Durmstrang, and Hogwarts—will all take part.

The whole school buzzes with excitement in anticipation of the arrival of the delegations for the tournament. Beauxbatons' representatives come in a house-sized, powder-blue, horse-drawn carriage drawn by a dozen enormous winged palominos that drink only single-malt whisky. Beauxbatons' chaperone, the elegant Madame Maxime, is as large as Hagrid, who immediately takes a liking to her. Durmstrang's delegates and their headmaster, Karkaroff, arrive on a magical ship that surfaces from the lake. A grand welcoming banquet is laid out in the great hall, where Hogwarts' own Dumbledore lays out the rules and introduces the

judges. The goblet of fire is placed in the entrance hall. All would-be contenders are invited to drop their names into the goblet, which will then choose a champion to represent each school. A thin, golden age line prevents students who are under the minimum age of seventeen from entering, although several try—with hairy results.

Following the Halloween feast, the goblet of fire spews forth the names of each school's designated champions: from Beauxbatons, Fleur Delacour; from Durmstrang, Viktor Krum; and from Hogwarts, Cedric Diggory. That should be all, but the goblet gives up yet another name—Harry Potter's! Harry becomes the fourth tournament contestant even though he is only fourteen and has no idea how his name got into the goblet of fire. Nobody believes that Harry did not somehow manage to enter on his own. Even Ron thinks Harry is just trying to show off, and doesn't speak to him for several weeks.

The first task of the tournament is scheduled for November 24. The contestants have no idea what to expect, except that it will test their courage in the face of the unknown. Hagrid gives Harry a hint, which he in turn shares with Cedric. The task involves dragons! It's a dangerous game, and Ron is so happy when Harry comes through alive that he sets aside his grudge.

The second task is scheduled for February 24, and in the meantime, school work keeps Harry busy. Hermoine starts a club called S.P.E.W. (the Society for the Promotion of Elfish Welfare) in an effort to get fair wages and working conditions for Hogwarts' house-elves. Then there's the Yule ball, which means Harry and Ron have to find dance partners. Ron has to wear his

musty old dress robes, and to make things worse, they're maroon—a colour he hates.

Cedric Diggory gives Harry a hint that the second task will involve an underwater challenge, and with the help of Moaning Myrtle the ghost and the house-elf Dobby, Harry prepares as best as he can. Prior to the third task on June 24, a series of strange events causes both Sirius Black and Albus Dumbledore to be concerned about Harry's safety. They are especially worried when Harry's scar pains him after a dream about Voldemort and Wormtail.

The third tournament task involves a maze, a sphinx, and a portkey that transports Harry and Cedric to the presence of none other than Voldemort. Once again, Harry does battle with the dark lord—and lives to tell the tale! Back at Hogwarts, Headmaster Dumbledore lays plans to diminish Voldemort's power. He resolves to establish an alliance with the giants and to banish the dementors from Azkaban. He also gets to the bottom of Harry's mysterious nomination as a tournament champion. Not surprisingly, people and circumstances are not what they seem.

Even though Voldemort is on the rise again, Harry must return to the Dursleys', as usual, at the end of the school term. On the way home on the Hogwarts Express, Harry gives George and Fred Weasley the thousand-galleon prize he won as the Triwizard Tournament champion. The twins will use it to start their own joke shop, but there's one proviso. They must promise to buy Ron some new dress robes and tell Ron the gift is from them.

WHO'S WHO
AND WHAT'S WHAT

(All definitions are based on the characters and references
in J.K. Rowling's original Harry Potter books.)

Accidental Magic Reversal Squad The agency responsible for reversing problems such as splinching, a complication that can result from the improper use of apparation. *See* **Apparition**, **Splinch** *and* **Obliviator**.

Accio The magic word used in the summoning charm.

Aging Potion As its name implies, this is a potion that makes its user look older.

Animagus (*pl.* **Animagi**) A witch or wizard who has the power to transform into an animal. Animagi must register with the Ministry of Magic, which tracks the animals they turn into and their distinctive markings. Only seven animagi have registered in the past century.

Apparate To instantly appear somewhere other than where you currently are. *See* **Apparition**.

Apparition Travelling by vanishing from one spot (disapparating) and instantly reappearing somewhere else (apparating). Only wizards who are of legal age and who have passed a test and been licensed by the Department of Magical Transportation are permitted to travel by this method. The process is very difficult and errors can result in complications such as splinching (leaving body parts behind). *See* **Apparate**, **Disapparate** *and* **Splinch**.

Archie An old wizard who attends the Quidditch World Cup in a long, flowery nightgown and won't be persuaded that his costume is not an appropriate muggle disguise for a male.

Avada Kedavra The killing curse, which is administered as a flash of blinding green light. The worst of the three unforgivable curses, it cannot be countered or blocked. This was the curse Voldemort used to kill James and Lily Potter. Harry is the only known survivor of the avada kedavra curse, and it is responsible for his lightening-bolt-shaped scar.

Avery A former member of Hogwarts' Slytherin House who supported Voldemort in the old days. When Voldemort was defeated, Avery pretended that he had been acting under the influence of the imperius curse.

Auror A dark-wizard-catcher.

Azkaban The wizard prison. Azkaban is fortress isolated on a tiny island and guarded by dementors.

Bagman, Ludovic (Ludo) Head of the Department of Magical Games and Sports. Bagman is a powerfully built, energetic, pot-bellied man with short blond hair, round blue eyes, and rosy cheeks. He once played quidditch for England, and was the best beater ever to play with the Wimbourne Wasps. Bagman is the commentator for the Quidditch World Cup, which he officiates in his old, black-and-yellow-striped Wasps robes.

In the old days, Ludo was implicated in a spying scheme orchestrated by Voldemort's follower Augustus Rookwood, but his name was cleared. He is a problem gambler who owes money to the goblins. He tries to earn enough to clear his debts by betting on Harry to win the Triwizard Tournament.

Bagman, Otto Ludo Bagman's brother, who gets into trouble for possession of a lawnmower with unusual powers. Arthur

Weasley helps Otto out of his predicament, and Ludo repays him by providing tickets for the Quidditch World Cup.

Banishing Charm The opposite of the summoning charm. It makes objects go away.

Bashir, Ali A foreign wizard who wants to export flying carpets to England, where he believes there is a niche market for family vehicles. Unfortunately, flying carpets have been banned in England, where they are defined as muggle artifacts by the Registry of Proscribed Charmable Objects.

Basil A tired, grumpy-looking Ministry of Magic wizard who is on duty during the Quidditch World Cup. Dressed in muggle disguise, Basil's job is to assign campsites to wizards arriving for the championship.

Basilisk An enormous snake born from a chicken's egg and hatched under a toad; also known as the king of serpents. The deadliest of all monsters, the basilisk has deadly fangs and can also kill its victims by petrifying them with a single glance.

Beater A quidditch position. A quidditch team has two beaters who protect their teammates from rocketing bludger balls. The beaters use a small club—like a baseball bat or a rounders bat—to knock the bludgers toward the opposing team.

Beauxbatons Academy of Magic One of the three major wizardry schools in Europe and a participant in the Triwizard Tournament. Beauxbatons' headmistress is Madame Olympe Maxime. She and her delegation arrive at Hogwarts in a house-sized, powder-blue, horse-drawn carriage pulled by a

dozen enormous, winged palominos that drink only single-malt whisky. The delegation is dressed in silk and shawls, and most members speak French. The palace at Beauxbatons is very elegant and the food is superb. Choirs of wood-nymphs serenade the students while they dine, and poltergeists are not allowed.

Binns, Professor A ghost who teaches Harry's boring History of Magic class at Hogwarts.

Black, Sirius James Potter's best friend, best man at James' and Lily's wedding, and Harry's godfather. Black is an unregistered animagus who has the ability to transform into huge black dog known to his friends as Padfoot. *See* **Snuffles**.

Blast-ended Skrewt *See* **Skrewt, Blast-ended**.

Bladvak A word that means pickaxe in the goblin language, Gobbledegook.

Bloody Baron A horrible, staring-eyed, gaunt-faced ghost whose robes are stained with silver blood. The Baron is Slytherin's resident ghost. He is the only one who can control the poltergeist Peeves.

Bludger One of the three types of balls used in quidditch. Bludger balls are jet black and slightly smaller than the red, soccer-ball-sized quaffle. Two bludger balls are required for a quidditch game. The bludgers are self-propelled and rocket around trying to get past the beaters to knock players off their brooms. They have never killed anyone at Hogwarts, although casualties have included several broken jaws.

Bluebottle A safe and reliable family broom advertised at the Quidditch World Cup. The Bluebottle has a built-in burglar alarm.

Bode and Croaker Unspeakables who work with the Department of Mysteries at the Ministry of Magic.

Boggart A shape-shifting creature that takes the form of whatever the person confronting it fears the most. Boggarts can be controlled by a laughter-inducing spell which causes them to shift from a terrible shape into a comical one. *See **Riddikulus***.

Boomslang Skin An ingredient in polyjuice potion.

Boris the Bewildered The figure memorialized in a statue located four doors to the right of the prefects' bathroom on the fifth floor of Hogwarts.

Brown, Lavender One of Harry's Gryffindor classmates. Lavender is a good friend of Parvinder Patil. Both girls are enthralled by Professor Trelawney's Divination class.

Bryce, Frank A war veteran with a stiff leg and low tolerance for noise and crowds. Bryce was the Riddles' gardener and was accused of their murders. He was taken to the police station at Great Hangletown, where he steadfastly maintained his innocence and claimed to have seen a pale, dark-haired, teenage boy trespassing on the grounds. Bryce was acquitted and continued to live in a run-down cottage on the Riddle estate. The new owner of the Riddle house paid him to do the gardening. When Bryce was killed by Voldemort, he was almost seventy-seven years old, very deaf, and suffering from chronic pain in his bad leg.

Bubble-head Charm A charm used by Fleur Delacour and Cedric Diggory in the second task of the Triwizard Tournament. The charm surrounded their heads with an enormous bubble inside which they could breathe.

Bubotuber A plant that looks like a huge, squirming black slug. Its shiny nodules are filled with thick, yellow-green pus that smells like gasoline. Diluted bubotuber pus is an excellent cure for acne. The pus is collected by squeezing the nodules. Dragonhide gloves must be worn to protect the skin.

Buckbeak (Bucky) A large, grey hippogriff that narrowly escapes execution by the Committee for the Disposal of Dangerous Creatures.

Bulgarian National Quidditch Team *(for the four hundred and twenty-second Quidditch World Cup)*. Team members include beaters Vulchanov and Volkov; chasers Dimitrov, Ivanova and Levski; keeper Zograf; and seeker Viktor Krum. Bulgaria's flag is red, green and white and the team wears scarlet uniforms. The team mascots are veela. Bulgaria loses the World Cup game to Ireland with a score of one hundred and sixty points, even though Krum captures the golden snitch.

Burrow, The The Weasleys' house in Ottery St. Catchpole.

Cadogan, Sir A squat, bumbling little knight in armour whose usual home is a painting in the north tower of Hogwarts castle.

Canary Cream A candy that turns whoever eats one into a huge canary. After a few minutes, the victim's feathers fall out and

he returns to normal. One of Fred and George Weasleys' inventions, Canary Creams sell for seven sickles apiece.

Chamber of Secrets A hidden chamber said to have been built at Hogwarts by Salazar Slytherin. According to legend, Slytherin sealed the chamber until such time as his "true heir" should arrive to open it and unleash its monster—a basilisk—to purge the school of muggle-born and mixed-blood students.

Chang, Cho The seeker and the only girl (a very pretty one) on Ravenclaw's quidditch team. Cho is a year ahead of Harry and a head shorter. She is Cedric Diggory's date at Hogwarts' Yule ball.

Chaser A quidditch position. A quidditch team has three chasers who score goals by getting the red quaffle ball through one of the three, fifty-foot-high golden hoops located at each end of the quidditch field. Each goal earns ten points.

Chinese Fireball A species of red dragon which has a fringe of gold spikes around its head and which shoots distinctive, mushroom-shaped fireballs.

Cobbing A quidditch foul that involves the excessive use of elbows.

Code of Wand Use Ministry of Magic regulations governing the use of wands. Clause three prohibits non-human creatures from carrying or using wands.

Committee on Experimental Charms A department in the Ministry of Magic; headed by Gilbert Wimple.

Common Welsh Green A wild dragon native to Britain.

Confundus Charm A charm used to make people believe something other than the truth. Individuals who are "confunded" (bewitched by this charm) are not responsible for their own actions.

Conjunctivitus Curse A curse that hurts its victim's eyes. Viktor Krum conquers his dragon with the help of this curse.

Crabbe Sr. Vincent's father, who is a death eater.

Crabbe, Vincent One of Draco Malfoy's muscular, thickset, mean-looking, brutish friends. Crabbe has a very thick neck and his hair looks like it was cut around a bowl. He is somewhat taller than his friend Goyle. Crabbe and Goyle are Draco Malfoy's faithful sidekicks. They are in the same year as Harry and they all belong to Slytherin House.

Crookshanks Hermione Granger's cat. Crookshanks is a large, fluffy, ginger-coloured animal with bowed legs, a squashed-looking, grumpy face and a tail that looks like a bottle brush.

Creevey, Colin A Hogwarts student who idolizes Harry and who is always following him around and trying to take his picture. Colin joins Gryffindor the year after Harry. His muggle father is a milkman.

Creevey, Dennis Colin's younger brother, who falls into the lake on his first journey to Hogwarts castle and is thrilled by the experience. Dennis belongs to Gryffindor House.

Croaker *See* **Bode and Croaker**.

Crouch Jr., Bartemius (Barty) A pale, fair-haired, slightly freckled man who is the son of Bartemius Sr. and a convicted supporter of Voldemort. Barty Jr. was accused of subjecting Frank Longbottom and his wife to the cruciatus curse. He was tried by his own father, convicted, and given a life sentence at Azkaban, where it was believed that he died. In reality, Barty's dying mother took his place at Azkaban and he was smuggled home, where his father used the imperius curse to control him. When Bertha Jorkins discovered the young Barty, his father (Crouch Sr.) administered an extra-strong memory charm to erase her memories.

When Book 4 begins, the house-elf Winky has persuaded Barty's father to let Barty wear an invisibility cloak and attend the Quidditch World Cup. It is Barty for whom Winky is "saving" a seat and it is Barty who steals Harry's wand and conjures the dark mark. Barty makes his way to Hogwarts and assists his master Voldemort in his plot to get Harry. He uses polyjuice potion to masquerade as Mad-Eye Moody, but his identity is eventually uncovered. Unfortunately, Cornelius Fudge orders the dementors to administer their kiss before Crouch can give evidence at a trial. *See* **Voldemort**.

Crouch Sr., Bartemius (Barty) Head of the Department of International Magical Co-operation and Percy Weasley's boss. Crouch is a stiff, upright, elderly man with short grey hair and a tidy little moustache. He speaks over two hundred languages, including Mermish, Gobbledegook, and Troll. Crouch is reputed to be even more obsessed with capturing dark wizards than Mad-Eye Moody. He is the former Head of the Department of Magical Law Enforcement, where he used particularly harsh measures to repress the followers of Voldemort. He gave aurors the authority to kill, approved the use of the unforgivable curses for law enforcement purposes, and imprisoned suspects without trial.

In Book 4, Wormtail and Voldemort imprison Barty Sr. with the imperius curse and release his son, who impersonates Mad-Eye Moody. Barty Sr. escapes and makes his way to Hogwarts, where his son kills him in the Forbidden Forest. *See* **Crouch Jr., Bartemius (Barty)** *and* **Weasley, Percy**.

Cruciatus Curse The torture curse; one of the three unforgivable curses.

Crucio The magic word used for the cruciatus curse.

Daily Mail A muggle newspaper.

Daily Prophet The wizards' newspaper. The paper also has an evening edition called the *Evening Prophet*.

Dark Forces, The: A Guide to Self-Protection The required text for fourth-year students taking Mad-Eye Moody's Defense Against the Dark Arts class at Hogwarts. Moody does not follow the text, preferring a more practical approach.

Dark Lord *See* **Voldemort**.

Dark Mark A colossal, glittering green skull with a tongue-like serpent sticking out of its mouth. The dark mark is Voldemort's sign and only his supporters know how to conjure it. In the

days of Voldemort's power, a dark mark would be floated in the sky whenever someone had been killed.

Voldemort's followers bear a tattoo-like image of the dark mark on their arms. This was burned into their flesh by their master, who uses it to summon them at will. When Voldemort touches the dark mark of any one of his death eaters, they are all expected to apparate at his side immediately.

Davies, Roger Captain of Ravenclaw's quidditch team during Harry's fourth year at Hogwarts, and Fleur Delacour's escort at the Yule ball.

De Mimsy-Porpington, Sir Nicholas The resident ghost of Gryffindor tower; also known as Nearly Headless Nick.

Death Eaters Supporters of Voldemort, who bear a tattoo-like image of his dark mark on their arms. When Voldemort was in power, his death eaters tortured and murdered great numbers of witches and wizards, conjuring a dark mark in the sky whenever they had killed. They also murdered muggles—just for fun. *See* **Dark Mark**.

Delacour, Fleur Beauxbatons' champion at the Triwizard Tournament. Fleur is a stunning blue-eyed beauty with waist-length, silvery-blonde hair. One of her grandmothers was a veela. Fleur's wand is a nine-and-a-half-inch specimen made from inflexible rosewood and a core of veela hair.

Delacour, Gabrielle Fleur's young sister, whom Harry rescues in the second task of the Triwizard Tournament.

Deletrius The magic word used to get rid of a magical image. Amos Diggory uses this word to get rid of the dark mark that appears when the *prior incantato* spell is used on Harry's wand.

Dementor A slimy, scabby, grey-skinned, eye-less creature whose breath rattles and whose normal costume is a face-concealing hooded cloak. Dementors guard the wizard prison at Azkaban. They are foul, evil, soul-less creatures which glorify decay and despair and drain all joy from those they encounter. Their victims are left with nothing but the memory of their own worst experiences, and most go mad within weeks. Albus Dumbledore fears that the dementors may be persuaded to join ranks with Voldemort. *See* **Dementor's Kiss**.

Dementor's Kiss A dementor's ultimate weapon, which can only be used with permission from the Ministry of Magic. A dementor's kiss sucks out its victim's soul, leaving behind a living but empty body that has been robbed of its memories and its sense of self.

Densaugeo The magic word used to cause a victim's teeth to grow like a beaver's.

Department for the Regulation and Control of Magical Creatures A department in the Ministry of Magic.

Department of International Magical Co-operation A Ministry of Magic department headed by Bartemius Crouch Sr. This department worked with the Department of Magical Games and Sports to arrange the Quidditch World Cup and the Triwizard Tournament.

Department of Magical Games and Sports The Ministry of Magic department that worked with the Department of International Magical Co-operation to arrange the Quidditch World Cup and the Triwizard Tournament. It is headed by Ludo Bagman.

Department of Magical Law Enforcement A Ministry of Magic department once headed by Bartemius Crouch.

Department of Mysteries A top-secret department at the Ministry of Magic. Department staff include unspeakables.

Diagon Alley A cobbled London street where witches and wizards do their shopping. Specialty shops on Diagon Alley include the Apothecary (for potion supplies), Madam Malkin's Robes for All Occasions, Eeylops Owl Emporium, Ollivanders (for wands), and Flourish and Blotts bookstore. The entrance to Diagon Alley is through a magical archway in the courtyard behind the Leaky Cauldron.

Diffindo The magic word Harry uses to split open Cedric Diggory's bag. This creates an opportunity to speak to Cedric in private and tell him about the dragons that will be used for the first tournament task.

Diggory, Amos A ruddy-faced, brown-bearded wizard who works for the Department for the Regulation and Control of Magical Creatures. Amos is Cedric Diggory's father.

Diggory, Cedric A tall, handsome Hufflepuff student who is appointed captain and seeker of his house quidditch team when Harry is in his third year at Hogwarts. Cedric is two years ahead of Harry. He is selected as the Hufflepuff champion for the Triwizard Tournament. His wand is twelve and a quarter inches of springy ash with a core of unicorn tail hair. Cedric is killed by Voldemort, but will always be remembered for his goodness, kindness and bravery.

Disapparate To instantly disappear from the place where you currently are. *See* **Apparate**, **Apparition**, *and* **Splinch**.

Disarming Spell A spell used to disarm a wizard by ejecting his wand from his possession. The magic word for the disarming spell is *expelliarmus*.

Dobby A house-elf who used to belong to the Malfoy family. Dobby was freed by his master and now works in a paid position at Hogwarts. *See* **House-elf**.

Dolohov, Antonin A supporter of Voldemort in the old days. Dolohov was apprehended by the Department of Magical Law Enforcement.

Dr. Filibuster's Fabulous Wet-Start, No-Heat Fireworks A special sort of indoor fireworks that creates long-lasting red and blue stars which ricochet off walls and ceilings.

Dragon A fantastic, fierce, fire-breathing winged creature that hatches from an egg. Dragons grow very quickly and cannot be tamed. Their eyes are their weakest point. Dragon breeding was outlawed by the Warlocks' Convention of 1709, but there are still two wild species in Britain—the common Welsh green and the Hebridean black. *See* **Chinese Fireball**, **Common Welsh Green**, **Hungarian Horntail**, *and* **Swedish Short-snout**.

Dumbledore, Aberforth Albus Dumbledore's brother, whose prosecution for performing inappropriate charms on a goat caused a scandal that was reported in all the papers of the day.

Dumbledore, Albus Headmaster of Hogwarts. Dumbledore is a tall, thin, blue-eyed old wizard with a crooked nose, long silver hair, and a long beard. Dumbledore wears half-moon spectacles; high-heeled, buckled boots; long robes; and purple cloak which sweeps the ground. Many consider him to be the greatest wizard of modern times.

Durmstrang A European wizardry school that does not admit muggle-born students and that teaches dark arts as part of its curriculum. Durmstrang's Triwizard Tournament competitors and their headmaster, Karkaroff, arrive in a ship which appears from the bottom of Hogwarts' lake. They wear matted fur cloaks and sleep on their ship. Durmstrang castle is a four-storey structure whose fires are lit only when needed for magical purposes. The grounds are very large and beautiful, although the students can only enjoy the mountains and lakes in the summer months, when there is enough daylight. Winter days at Durmstrang are very short.

Dursley, Dudley The muggle son of Petunia and Vernon Dursley and Harry Potter's cousin. Dudley is a porky, pink-faced, fat-headed boy with small, watery blue eyes and smooth, blond hair. Dudley goes to Smeltings Secondary School.

Dursley, Petunia Dudley's mother and wife of Vernon. Petunia Dursley is Harry's muggle aunt on his mother's side; Lily Potter was her sister. Petunia is a thin, bony, horse-faced blonde with an unusually long neck that comes in handy for spying on her neighbours.

Dursley, Vernon Dudley's muggle father; married to Harry's Aunt Petunia. Vernon Dursley is a big, beefy, purple-faced fellow with a very large black moustache and hardly any neck. Vernon works as a director at Grunnings, a local drill-manufacturing firm.

Elf *See* **House-elf.**

Enervate The magic word used to restore someone to consciousness.

Engorgement Charm A charm that is used to blow things up to maximum size. Hagrid grows boulder-sized pumpkins with the aid of an engorgement charm. The Weasley twins use it to make Ton-Tongue Toffee. The words *engorgio* and *reducio* are used to activate and reverse the charm.

Engorgio The magic word used to activate an engorgement charm.

Errol The Weasley family's elderly, feeble, grey owl.

Evening Prophet The evening edition of the wizards' newspaper, *Daily Prophet*.

Expecto Patronum The magic words used for the patronus charm.

Expelliarmus The magic word for the disarming spell, which is used to eject a wand from another wizard's possession.

Exploding Snap A card game.

Fang Hagrid's huge black boarhound. Fang is far less ferocious than he looks.

Fat Friar One of Hogwarts' resident ghosts. The friar is a former student of Hufflepuff House.

Fat Lady A very fat woman in a pink silk dress whose portrait guards the entrance to Gryffindor House.

Fawkes Dumbledore's pet phoenix.

Filch, Argus Hogwarts' bulgy-eyed, ill-tempered caretaker. Filch and his cat, Mrs. Norris, patrol the hallways and try to catch students who are breaking the rules.

Finite Incantarum The magic words which stop the effect of a previous enchantment.

Firebolt A very expensive, state-of-the-art flying-broom designed for racing. The Firebolt has a polished ash handle, a broomtail made from specially selected birch twigs, and an unbreakable braking charm. It accelerates from zero to one hundred and fifty miles (over two hundred and forty kilometres) per hour in just ten seconds. Each Firebolt has a unique registration number that is applied by hand.

Fletcher, Mundungus A troublesome old wizard who once tried to hex Arthur Weasley when his back was turned. Fletcher sues the Ministry of Magic for compensation when his property is ruined at the Quidditch World Cup. He claims the loss of a twelve-bedroom suite and jacuzzi, when in fact, his tent was just a cloak propped on sticks.

Flitwick, Professor Hogwarts' Charms teacher. Professor Flitwick is so tiny that he has to stand on a pile of books to see over his desk.

Flobberworm A rather boring magical creature which flourishes best if it is left alone.

Floo Network A network that connects wizard fireplaces to facilitate travel between them. Muggle fireplaces are normally not connected to the network, although the Floo Regulation Panel sometimes makes exceptions.

Floo Powder A sparkling powder that facilitates travelling from one wizard fire to another.

Foe-glass A type of dark-arts-detector that looks like a mirror, but reflects what is *outside* the room in which it is located.

Forbidden Forest A forest on the grounds of Hogwarts. It is off limits to students because it is full of dangerous beasts.

Fortescue, Florean The wizard who runs the ice cream parlour in Diagon Alley. Fortescue is an expert in medieval witch-burning.

Four-point Spell A spell that makes a wizard's wand point due north so that it can be used to check direction, like a compass.

Fridwulfa Hagrid's mother, who abandons him to the care of his muggle father when Hagrid is about three. Fridwulfa is a giantess. She is one of the last of her kind to live in Britain. *See* **Giant**.

Fudge, Cornelius Head of the Ministry of Magic. Fudge is a portly little man who likes to wear pinstriped suits, coats or cloaks; a scarlet tie; a lime-green bowler hat; and pointed purple boots.

Furnunculus The magic word used to inflict boils on a victim.

Galleon A gold coin used as wizard money. There are seventeen silver sickles or four hundred and ninety-three bronze knuts to a gold galleon.

Giant A twenty-foot-tall creature that has a reputation for viciousness and for enjoying killing. Britain's giants were already dying out when aurors began to hunt them down. A few survivors may still live in the mountain regions of other countries.

Gillyweed A plant that resembles slimy, grey-green rattails and has a rubbery texture. The person who eats it temporarily grows gills and flippers that facilitate breathing and swimming under water.

Gladrags Wizardwear A wizard apparel shop with outlets in Paris, London and Hogsmeade. One of the advertisers at the Quidditch World Cup.

Gnome A small, leathery, not-too-bright creature with horny little feet, sharp teeth and a bumpy bald head. Gnomes live in holes in people's gardens.

Gobbledegook The language spoken by goblins.

Goblet of Fire A large, crudely hewn wooden cup filled with dancing, blue-white flames. The goblet is stored in a large, old-looking, jewel-encrusted wood casket. Prospective contestants in the Triwizard Tournament write their names on slips of paper and drop them into the goblet, which selects the most worthy champion to represent each school. Candidates who place their names into the goblet are obligated to see things through

to the end, and may not drop out of the tournament. A thin, golden, age line prevents candidates under the compulsory age of seventeen from approaching the goblet.

Goblin A small, swarthy creature with a clever face, pointed beard, and very long fingers and feet. Goblins run Gringotts, the wizards' bank, and are not to be messed with. Their language is called Gobbledegook.

Goblin Liaison Office A department of the Ministry of Magic; headed by Cuthbert Mockridge.

Gobstones A game played much like marbles, except that when players lose points, the gobstones squirt a smelly liquid into their faces.

Godric's Hollow Where Harry lived with his parents, Lily and James Potter, until they were killed by Voldemort.

Golden Snitch The most important of the three types of balls used in quidditch. The tiny, bright-gold snitch has fluttering silver wings. It is only the size of a walnut and therefore very hard to see and catch. When the seeker succeeds in catching the snitch, the team earns one hundred and fifty points and the match ends.

Goyle Sr. Gregory's father, who is a death eater.

Goyle, Gregory One of Draco Malfoy's thickset, mean-looking, brutish friends. Malfoy and his sidekicks, Crabbe and Goyle, are in the same year as Harry. They all belong to Slytherin House. Goyle suffers a bad case of boils when a furnunculus spell is misdirected. *See* **Malfoy, Draco**.

Granger, Hermione A Gryffindor who is best friends with Harry Potter and Ron Weasley. Hermione is an excellent student even though her parents (both dentists) are muggles. Hermione has a bossy voice and her brown hair is usually bushy unless she takes the time to tame it with Sleekeazy's Hair Potion. Until her fourth year at Hogwarts, her front teeth are rather large, but she takes advantage of a misdirected *densaugeo* command to reduce their size.

Hermione launches the Society for the Promotion of Elfish Welfare (S.P.E.W.) in an effort to better the lot of house-elves. She is not very successful because house-elves prefer work to freedom, and they *like* serving even ungrateful masters. Hermione makes friends with the Durmstrang champion, Viktor Krum, and accompanies him to the Yule ball in periwinkle-blue robes. Her name is pronounced Her-MY-oh-nee, but in Viktor's Bulgarian accent, it comes out as Hermy-own-ninny.

Great Hall A huge, grand room where Hogwarts school ceremonies and assemblies are held. The ceiling is bewitched to look like the sky, and at night, its velvety blackness is dotted with stars.

Great Hangleton The town neighbouring Little Hangleton. Frank Bryce is taken to Great Hangleton for interrogation by the police.

Gregorovitch A noted wand-maker whose preferred stylings are distinctly different from Mr. Ollivander's.

Grindylow A sharp-horned, green water demon whose strong, long fingers are very brittle. Grindylows can be overcome by breaking their grip.

Gringotts The wizards' goblin-run bank, which is heavily protected by spells and enchantments.

Grubbly-Plank, Professor A big-chinned witch with short grey hair who takes over the Care of Magical Creatures class when Hagrid is indisposed.

Hagrid, Rubeus Keeper of Keys and Grounds at Hogwarts. Hagrid is a soft-hearted giant of a man—twice as tall and five times as wide as a normal person. He is a muscular, wild-looking fellow with beetle-black eyes, shaggy black hair, and a beard that hides most of his face. Hagrid's mother was the giantess Fridwulfa, who abandoned him when he was about three. He was raised by his muggle father, who died when Hagrid was a boy. Hagrid is a notoriously bad cook who is especially fond of large, rather dangerous animals. A former Hogwarts student, he lives in a cottage at the edge of the Forbidden Forest and teaches Care of Magical Creatures.

Hanged Man, The The village pub in Little Hangleton.

Hawkshead Attacking Formation A quidditch manoeuvre used in the four hundred and twenty-second Quidditch World Cup.

Hedwig Harry's snowy owl.

Hermes Percy Weasley's owl.

Hinkypunk A small, frail, seemingly harmless one-legged creature that resembles wisps of smoke. Hinkypunks use lanterns to lure wayward travellers into bogs.

Hippogriff A bizarre, orange-eyed creature with the hindquarters of a horse and the long-taloned, cruel-beaked, winged front body of a giant eagle. To approach a hippogriff safely, it is necessary to maintain eye contact and bow. It is not safe to proceed until the hippogriff bows back.

Hogsmeade The only British settlement whose inhabitants are all witches and wizards. Hogsmeade is home to a number of specialty shops, including Dervish and Banges, which carries wizardry supplies; the Three Broomsticks pub, renowned for its butterbeer; Zonko's Joke Shop; and Honeydukes, the famous candy store.

Hogwarts Express The scarlet steam engine that transports students to and from Hogwarts each term. The train leaves from platform nine and three-quarters at London's King's Cross station at precisely 11 o'clock every September 1.

Hogwarts School of Witchcraft and Wizardry One of the finest schools of wizardry in the world, Hogwarts is situated atop a high mountain on the shore of a great black lake inhabited by a giant squid. The forest on the grounds is full of dangerous beasts and is forbidden territory to all pupils. Hogwarts castle is protected by a variety of enchantments and it is considered one of the safest places on earth. Its location is invisible to muggles.

Hogwarts was founded over a thousand years ago by Godric Gryffindor, Helga Hufflepuff, Rowena Ravenclaw and Salazar Slytherin—the four greatest wizards and witches of their age. Each of the founders established a house and chose students who exemplified the virtues they valued most. Today, a sorting hat is used for this purpose. It takes seven years to complete the Hogwarts course of studies.

Hooch, Madam Hogwarts' teacher of broom-flying. Madam has short, grey hair and yellow, hawk-like eyes.

House-elf A rather ugly, doll-sized creature with a long, thin nose; bat-like ears; enormous, tennis-ball-sized eyes; and a high-pitched voice. House-elves are usually owned by wealthy old wizarding families. They are unswervingly loyal to their masters.

Howler A scalding letter that is delivered by owl post. It begins to scream and yell as soon as it is opened. A howler that is not opened immediately will explode.

Hungarian Horntail A huge, fierce, lizard-like black dragon with scaly skin and a deadly, spiked tail. Horntails are among the most vicious of dragons and they can shoot fire at a range of forty feet—twice as far as most other dragon species.

Impedimenta The magic word used for the impediment jinx.

Impediment Jinx A spell that uses the word *impedimenta* to deter and obstruct attackers.

Imperius Curse One of the three unforgivable curses. The imperius curse gives a wizard total control over his victim. Voldemort controlled many witches and wizards with this curse, making it difficult for the Ministry of Magic to determine who was being forced to commit crimes and who was acting freely. Only wizards with unusual strength of character are able to withstand the curse. For most, avoidance is the best remedy.

Imperio The magic word used for the imperius curse.

Improper Use of Magic Office A department in the Ministry of Magic. One of its duties is to ensure that underage wizards do not perform spells outside of school.

Incendio The magic word Arthur Weasley uses to light a fire in the Dursleys' fireplace.

Invisibility Cloak A magical cloak that makes its wearer invisible.

Irish National Quidditch Team *(for the four hundred and twenty-second Quidditch World Cup)*. Team members include beaters Connolly and Quigley; keeper Ryan; chasers Troy, Mullet and Moran; and seeker Aidan Lynch. The team wears green uniforms embroidered in silver and flies on Firebolts. The team mascots are leprechauns. Ireland wins the Quidditch World Cup with a ten-point lead over Bulgaria.

Jelly-legs Jinx A spell that causes its victim's legs to wobble.

Jorkins, Bertha A Ministry of Magic employee who works in the Department of Magical Games and Sports. Bertha is renowned for her bad memory and her terrible sense of direction. It turns out that her bad memory is the result of the senior Bartemius Crouch's overzealousness in applying a memory charm when Bertha discovers the truth about his son. Poor Bertha has the misfortune of running into Wormtail while she is on vacation in Albania. She is taken to his master, Voldemort, who interrogates and then kills her. *See* **Crouch Jr., Bartemius**.

Kappa A creepy, web-handed, water-dwelling creature that resembles a scaly monkey. Kappas strangle unfortunate swimmers who

venture into their territory. They are commonly found in Mongolia.

Karkaroff, Igor The headmaster at Durmstrang and chaperone of the visiting delegation. Professor Karkaroff is a tall, thin, oily voiced man with short white hair and a goatee that ends in a curl. He is a former death eater who has done time at Azkaban. He cuts a deal with the Ministry of Magic and is released in exchange for identifying other supporters of Voldemort. Among those he names are Antonin Dolohov, Evan Rosier, Travers, Mulciber, Augustus Rookwood and Severus Snape.

Keeper A quidditch position. The keeper tries to stop the other team's chasers from getting the quaffle ball through the hoops in a quidditch match.

Knut A small bronze coin used as wizard money. There are twenty-nine bronze knuts to a silver sickle.

Krum, Viktor Seeker and star player on Bulgaria's national quidditch team. Viktor is a thin, dark, sallow-skinned youth with heavy black eyebrows and a big hooked nose. He is an exceptional flyer who is a master of the Wronski Feint, and is only eighteen when he plays in the Quidditch World Cup. Viktor is selected as the Durmstrang champion for the Triwizard Tournament. His wand is a Gregorovitch creation made from rigid, thick, ten-and-a-quarter-inch hornbeam with a dragon core. Viktor and Hermione Granger become good friends, and Viktor invites Hermione to visit him in Bulgaria. *See* **Granger, Hermione**.

Leaky Cauldron A tiny, inconspicuous, grubby-looking London pub which is invisible to muggles. The pub serves as the entrance to Diagon Alley, where many wizard shops are found.

Leaving Feast The end-of-term wind-up dinner at Hogwarts.

Leprechaun A little bearded man who wears a red vest and carries a tiny green or gold lamp. Leprechauns serve as mascots for the Irish national team. At the Quidditch World Cup, they marched into the stadium in shamrock formation and tossed fistfuls of gold into the stands. Unfortunately, leprechaun gold vanishes within a few hours.

Lestrange The surname of a husband and wife—both former members of Hogwarts' Slytherin House—who supported Voldemort in the old days and are currently imprisoned at Azkaban.

Little Hangleton The village in which the Riddle house and The Hanged Man pub are located.

Lockhart, Gilderoy The incompetent dandy who teaches Defence Against the Dark Arts in Harry's second year at Hogwarts.

Longbottom, Frank Neville's father and a former auror. After Voldemort's downfall, his followers, including young Barty Crouch, tortured Frank and his wife with the cruciatus curse in an attempt to get information about their master's whereabouts. The Longbottoms went mad and are now residents of St. Mungo's Hospital for Magical Maladies and Injuries. Neville and his grandmother visit them, but Frank and his wife do not recognize them.

Longbottom, Neville One of Harry's Gryffindor classmates. Round-faced, accident-prone, forgetful Neville lives with his eccentric grandmother, who is delighted when he finally shows some aptitude for wizardry at the age of eight. Neville has a remembrall to help him remember things, but he is still forgetful and not very good at Charms or Potions. Herbology is his best subject.

Lumos The magic word that causes the end of a wizard's wand to light up. The spell is reversed by uttering the word *nox*.

Lupin, Remus J. Defence Against the Dark Arts professor during Harry's third year at Hogwarts. Lupin is a werewolf who is able to control his condition with the help of wolfsbane potion. He is a sick- and tired-looking young man who dresses rather shabbily and whose light-brown hair shows signs of grey. Lupin is a former Hogwarts student whose best friends were James Potter, Sirius Black, and Peter Pettigrew.

Macnair, Walden An executioner employed by the Committee for the Disposal of Dangerous Creatures. Macnair is a death eater.

Mad-Eye Moody *See* **Moody, Alastor**.

Magical Mediterranean Water-Plants and Their Properties A book that "Professor Moody" (Barty Crouch Jr. in disguise) lends Neville Longbottom in the hope that Harry will use it to master the second task of the Triwizard Tournament.

Malfoy, Draco A conceited, sneaky bully whom Harry hates even more than his porky cousin Dudley. Malfoy has a pale, pointed face. He belongs to Slytherin House and is rarely seen without

his brutish sidekicks, Crabbe and Goyle. Malfoy and his Slytherin cronies wear "Potter Stinks" badges when Harry is selected as a champion in the Triwizard Tournament.

Like the rest of his family, Malfoy believes that only pure-blood wizards should be allowed to study magic. When he insults the muggle-born Hermione Granger, Harry casts a furnunculus spell which is misdirected and hits Goyle by mistake. Goyle suffers a bad case of boils, while Hermione's teeth grow like a beaver's when the densaugeo spell Draco aims at Harry hits her instead.

Malfoy, Lucius Draco's father. Lucius is a former supporter of Voldemort. He makes a show of abandoning the dark arts after his master is overthrown, but his true allegiance is suspect. Lucius is responsible for organizing the torture of the muggle Roberts family after the Quidditch World Cup. *See* **Roberts, Mr**.

Malfoy, Narcissa Draco's mother and wife of Lucius' wife. Narcissa is a tall, thin blonde whose good looks are marred by her habit of looking like she is smelling something nasty.

Marauder's Map, The A magical map created by James Potter (Prongs), Remus Lupin (Moony), Sirius Black (Padfoot) and Peter Pettigrew (Wormtail) when the four were students at Hogwarts. The map details the whole of Hogwarts' school and grounds and shows the identity, location and movements of anyone who is inside Hogwarts.

Maxime, Olympe The headmistress at Beauxbatons and chaperone of the visiting delegation. Madame Maxime is an attractive,

dark-eyed, olive-skinned woman with sleek black hair and a somewhat beaky nose. She is as tall as Hagrid, but is very sensitive about her giant blood and claims that she is just big-boned. Madame usually wears black satin adorned with opals.

McGonagall, Minerva Professor, deputy headmistress, and head of Gryffindor House. McGonagall is a tall, severe-looking woman who favours emerald-green robes and cloaks. She wears square eyeglasses and pulls her black hair back into a tight bun. She teaches transfiguration and can change shape at will.

Mediwizard The wizards' equivalent of a paramedic. A mediwizard "treats" referee Mostafa with a swift kick to the shins when he is temporarily bewitched by a veela during the Quidditch World Cup.

Memory Charm A charm that erases memories. It is frequently used on muggles who have witnessed wizard phenomena they should not have seen. Memory modification can be a somewhat disorienting experience. The magic word used for the memory charm is *obliviate*.

Mermish The language of the merpeople.

Merpeople Grey-skinned, yellow-eyed, spear-carrying water creatures with silver fish tails, wild green hair and broken teeth. Merpeople live in the lake in front of Hogwarts Castle. They wear thick, pebble necklaces and keep grindylows for pets.

Ministry of Magic A multi-department agency headed by Cornelius Fudge. One of the ministry's roles is keeping muggles

unaware that there are witches and wizards everywhere. The ministry also regulates underage wizards, experimental charms, magical creatures, international relations, magical games and sport, and the improper use of magic.

Moaning Myrtle A ghost who haunts a toilet in the girl's first-floor bathroom at Hogwarts. Fifty years ago, Myrtle met her death when she encountered the dreaded basilisk in the bathroom she now haunts.

Mockridge, Cuthbert Head of the Goblin Liaison Office at the Ministry of Magic.

Moody, Alastor (Mad-Eye) An eccentric retired wizard who was the best auror of his time. His motto is "constant vigilance." Moody's face bears the marks of his battles and every inch seems scarred. A chunk of nose is missing (*see* **Rosier, Evan**) and his mouth is a slanted gash. He has long grey hair and frightening eyes. One is small and beady, while the other eye is large, round and electric-blue. It continually moves— independently of its mate—and can see through invisibility cloaks. Moody has a wooden leg that ends in a clawed foot. He is an old friend of Albus Dumbledore, and as a special favour, has come out of retirement to teach the Defense Against the Dark Arts class. Shortly before he is due to leave for his term at Hogwarts, he is captured by Bartemius Crouch Jr. and locked away in an enchanted trunk. Crouch assumes Moody's identity with the aid of polyjuice potion made with the old auror's hair. Rather than sticking to the prescribed curriculum, which deals with counter-curses, Moody (Crouch Jr.) teaches his students about illegal, dark curses—ostensibly

so that they will be prepared to deal with them. The real Moody is eventually discovered with the aid of veritaserum.

Morsmordre The magic word used to summon the dark mark. *See* **Voldemort** *and* **Dark Mark**.

Mostafa, Hassan Chairwizard of the International Association of Quidditch and referee for the Quidditch World Cup. Mostafa hails from Egypt. He is a small, skinny, bald wizard with a huge moustache. He wears pure gold robes and uses a silver whistle. *See* **Mediwizard**.

Mrs. Skower's All-Purpose Magical Mess-Remover A product advertised at the Quidditch World Cup. Mrs. Skower's motto is "No Pain, No Stain!"

Mudblood An insulting name for a witch or wizard who has non-magic (muggle) parents.

Muggle A non-magic person.

Muggle-repelling Charm As its name implies, a charm used to keep muggles away. Every inch of the stadium at which the Quidditch World Cup was held was treated with muggle-repelling charms.

Murcus The ferocious-looking chieftainess of the merpeople.

Nearly Headless Nick *See* **De Mimsy-Porpington, Sir Nicholas**.

Nagini A huge, twelve-foot-long, diamond-backed snake whose venom is milked to provide sustenance for Voldemort.

N.E.W.T. A Nastily Exhausting Wizarding Test; Hogwarts' highest qualification.

Niffler A long-snouted, fluffy black creature with flat, spadelike front paws that are useful for digging. Nifflers like sparkly things and are most often found in mines.

Norris, Mrs. Mr. Filch's scrawny, bulgy-eyed, dust-coloured cat. She patrols the halls of Hogwarts and reports to Filch if she sees anyone misbehaving.

Nott A death eater.

Nox The magic word that ends the *lumos* spell and snuffs out a lighted wand.

Obliviate The magic word for the memory charm.

Obliviator An employee of the Accidental Magic Reversal Squad.

Ogg The Hogwarts gamekeeper before Hagrid.

Ollivanders A wand shop located in Diagon Alley. The Ollivanders have been makers of fine wands since 382 BC. "The wand chooses the wizard," according to Mr. Ollivander, who conducts the Weighing of the Wands ceremony at the Triwizard Tournament. Wands are made with a powerful magical core and no two are quite the same. The core of Voldemort's thirteen-and-a-half-inch yew wand is a feather from the phoenix Fawkes. Harry's eleven-inch holly wand contains the only other feather Fawkes has ever given. When wands which share the same core duel, priori incantatem results: one wand forces the other to replay the spells it has performed in reverse order.

Omnioculars A gadget that looks like a pair of brass binoculars with extra dials and knobs that can replay or slow down

action, or offer a play-by-play breakdown of whatever is being viewed. Omnioculars sell for ten galleons a pair at the Quidditch World Cup.

Ottery St. Catchpole The village where the Weasleys live.

O.W.L. Ordinary Wizarding Level examinations taken by Hogwarts students when they are fifteen (in their fifth year).

Owlery A cold, draughty, circular stone room at the top of Hogwarts' west tower. The floor is lined with straw and the room is fitted with perches for the hundreds of owls that come and go through the unglazed windows.

Parselmouth Someone who has the ability to talk to snakes. Salazar Slytherin was a famous parselmouth, which is why the symbol of Slytherin House is a snake.

Parseltongue The language used by snakes.

Patronus A guardian conjured by the patronus charm. A patronus creates a shield of positive forces that can protect against dementors.

Patronus Charm A very difficult advanced charm used to conjure a patronus. The charm requires concentrating on a single, very happy memory while uttering the words *"expecto patronum."*

Patil, Parvati One of Harry's Gryffindor classmates. Parvati's twin sister, Padma, is also a Hogwarts student. Parvati and Lavender Brown are good friends, and both girls are enthralled by Professor Trelawney's Divination class. Parvati is Harry Potter's date at the Yule ball.

Patil, Padma Parvati's twin sister, who is a member of Ravenclaw. Padma is Ron Weasley's date at the Yule ball.

Payne, Mr. The site manager of the Quidditch World Cup campground in the second field. This is where the Diggory family camps.

Peasegood, Arnold An obliviator with the Accidental Magic Reversal Squad.

Peeves A wicked poltergeist who haunts Hogwarts. Peeves wears an orange bow tie and a bell-covered hat. He delights in nasty mischief of all sorts. Only the Bloody Baron can control him.

Pensieve A carved, shallow stone basin that holds a bright, swirling, silver-white substance. The pensieve is used to store excess thoughts until such time as they can be studied at leisure.

Perkins An old warlock who is Arthur Weasley's colleague in the Misuse of Muggle Artifacts Office at the Ministry of Magic. Perkins lends Arthur the tent the Weasleys use at the Quidditch World Cup.

Pettigrew, Peter A short, once plump, balding man with a pointed nose and small, watery eyes. Pettigrew was a close friend of James Potter, Remus Lupin and Sirius Black while the four were students at Hogwarts. Like James and Sirius, he became an animagus. He could take the shape of a rat that his friends called Wormtail. Pettigrew was James and Lily Potters' secret-keeper. He betrayed their whereabouts to Voldemort and framed Sirius Black for the murders that sent him to Azkaban. After his dark master's downfall, he went into hiding

as Ron Weasley's rat, Scabbers. When his identity was discovered, he returned to active service on behalf of Voldemort.

Philosopher's Stone A legendary, blood-red stone created by the noted alchemist Nicolas Flamel. The stone can change base metals to gold and produce the elixir of life, which grants immortality to anyone who drinks it. Also known as the sorcerer's stone.

Phoenix A remarkable, swan-sized bird that bursts into flame when it is time for it to die, and is reborn from its own ashes. Phoenixes have glorious red and gold plumage and golden talons. Their tears have the power to heal, and they can carry very heavy loads. They make extremely faithful pets.

Pig Short for Pigwidgeon. Pig is the highly excitable, palm-sized grey owl Ron Weasley receives as a gift from Sirius Black.

Pigwidgeon Ron Weasley's owl, who is named by Ron's sister Ginny. *See* **Pig**.

Pince, Madam Hogwarts' thin, irritable librarian, who looks a bit like a vulture.

Polyjuice Potion A complicated potion that, for a short time, transforms the person who drinks it into someone else. Polyjuice takes a month to prepare. It requires lacewing flies that have been stewed for twenty-one days, leeches, fluxweed picked at the full moon, knotgrass, powdered bicorn horn, shredded boomslang skin, and a bit of whoever you want to transform into. The recipe can be found in the book *Most Potente Potions*.

Porskoff Ploy A quidditch strategy used in the four hundred and twenty-second World Cup.

Portkey An enchanted, unobtrusive object used to transport wizards from place to place at prearranged times. Portkeys usually look like ordinary litter so that muggles will not be tempted to pick them up. They can be used to transport large groups at one time. Two hundred portkeys were placed at strategic points around the country to transport wizards to the Quidditch World Cup.

Potter, Harry Born on July 31, Harry is the orphaned son of James and Lily Potter, who are killed by the wicked, powerful Voldemort when Harry is just a year old. Harry lives with his only relatives, Vernon and Petunia Dursley and their young son Dudley. The Dursleys are muggles (non-magic folk) who despise wizards, but an ancient magic protects Harry while he is in their care.

Harry wears round glasses. He has his father's unruly, jet-black hair and his mother's green eyes. He is small and skinny with a thin face and rather knobby knees. His most distinguishing feature is the thin, lightning-bolt-shaped scar on his forehead. This is the legacy of Voldemort's unsuccessful attempt to kill him when he was a baby. Harry is the only wizard ever to have survived an attack by Voldemort. *See also:* **Ollivanders** *and* **Voldemort**.

Potter, James and Lily Harry's parents, both of whom were powerful wizards. Lily and James were killed by the evil Voldemort on Halloween night when Harry was one year old, but Lily managed to protect her son. James Potter was an unregistered animagus who could take the shape of a stag known to his friends as Prongs. The Potters lived at Godric's Hollow.

Prior Incantanto The magic words that cause a wand to reveal the last spell it performed. A wizard who wishes to use this spell must place his own wand tip against the tip of the wand being tested.

Priori Incantantem The reverse spell effect. *See* **Ollivanders**.

Pringle, Apollyon The Hogwarts caretaker in the days when Arthur and Molly Weasley were students there.

Quaffle One of the three types of balls used in quidditch. The bright-red quaffle is about the size of a soccer ball. Ten points are earned each time a chaser manages to get the quaffle through one of the opposing team's hoops.

Quick-quotes Quill A long, acid-green quill that has the ability to write notes down by itself.

Quidditch This is the wizards' national sport, which is played on flying broomsticks. There are seven hundred ways to commit a quidditch foul. There are seven players on a quidditch team: three chasers, two beaters, a keeper, and a seeker. A quidditch field (also called a pitch) has three fifty-foot-high golden hoops at each end The chasers try to get the red, soccer-ball-sized quaffle through the hoops to score ten points. The keeper tries to prevent the opposing team from scoring. The keeper is assisted by two black bludger balls which rocket around trying to knock players off their brooms. The beaters knock

the bludgers away with small clubs that look like baseball or rounders bats. The seeker chases the tiny, silver-winged golden snitch, which is very hard to see and catch. (The record is three months.) Capturing the snitch earns one hundred and fifty points and ends the game. The game is not over until the snitch has been caught.

Quidditch World Cup   The annual, international quidditch championship. The four hundred and twenty-second World Cup takes place in Britain. This is the first time in thirty years that Britain has hosted the event, and tickets are extremely hard to come by. The World Cup is attended by over one hundred thousand wizards from all around the world. They arrive by apparating, by regular muggle public transport, and by using one of the two hundred portkeys that have been placed at strategic points around the country.

Quietus   The magic word used to return a magically enhanced loud voice back to its normal volume.

Rebirthing Party   The ceremony at which Voldemort regains his power.

Red Cap   A nasty, goblin-like creature that lurks in dungeons, battle fields, and other areas where blood has been shed. Red caps lay in wait to bludgeon travellers who have lost their way.

Reducio   The magic word that counteracts the engorgement charm.

Reducto   The magic word used for the reductor curse.

Reductor Curse   A curse used to blast solid objects out of the way. It does not work on transitory objects like mists. The reductor curse uses the magic word *reducto*.

Registry of Proscribed Charmable Objects   A division of the Ministry of Magic which deals with banned muggle artifacts.

Relashio   The magic word Harry tries when he wants his wand to shoot sparks at the grindylows he encounters during the second task of the Triwizard Tournament. Instead, the wand sends jets of boiling water which appear to scald the creatures.

Reparo   The magic word used to repair things.

Riddikulus   The magic word used against boggarts. Its effectiveness requires intense concentration to conjure an amusing image. The boggart takes the shape of this image and is destroyed by the resulting laughter.

Riddle House   A run-down old house on a hill overlooking the village of Little Hangleton. Local residents still refer to it as "the Riddle house," even though it has been fifty years since any Riddles lived there. Once a grand, well-kept manor, the house has been mostly uninhabited since the time when a maid discovered the snobbish Mr. and Mrs. Riddle and their son Tom murdered in their drawing room, all three looking as if they had been scared to death. The gardener, Frank Bryce, was accused of the murders but eventually acquitted. The current owner is a wealthy man who keeps the house for tax purposes and keeps Bryce on as the gardener. *See* **Bryce, Frank**.

Riddle, Tom Marvolo   A student at Hogwarts fifty years before Harry's time. Tom's mother was a witch who named him for his muggle father (Tom Sr.) and grandfather. She died just after Tom was born and he was raised in an orphanage. The true heir of Slytherin, Tom opened chamber of secrets and released the fearsome basilisk that killed Moaning Myrtle. His name, Tom Marvolo Riddle, is an anagram for the words "I am Lord Voldemort." Tom Riddle is none other than the dark lord himself. *See* **Voldemort**.

Riddle, Tom Sr. Voldemort's muggle father.

Roberts, Mr. The muggle site manager of the Quidditch World Cup campground in the first field, where Harry, Hermione and the Weasleys camp. Mr. Roberts doesn't know what to make of all the "weirdos" visiting his campground, even though he gets ten memory charms a day to erase his recollections of his most bizarre encounters with wizards. He and his family fall victim to a gang of suspected death eaters who hide their identity behind hoods. *See* **Death Eaters** *and* **Malfoy, Lucius**.

Rookwood, Augustus A Department of Mysteries employee who supported Voldemort in the old days and served as his spy. Rockwood was able to pass on information within the Ministry of Magic itself. He even used Ludo Bagman (in the days when Ludo was a quidditch player) to collect information for him.

Rosier, Evan A former member of Hogwarts' Slytherin House who supported Voldemort in the old days. He was killed by Mad-Eye Moody when the latter was an auror. Moody lost part of his nose in the struggle.

Rosmerta, Madam The pretty, curvaceous barmaid at the Three Broomsticks pub in Hogsmeade.

Rowling, J.K. Joanne Kathleen (Jo) Rowling, author of the Harry Potter series. Rowling was born in Chipping Sodbury in the UK in 1965. She studied French at the University of Exeter in Devon. She later taught French in Edinburgh, where she currently lives with her daughter.

St. Mungo's Hospital for Magical Maladies and Injuries The wizards' hospital, where Frank Longbottom and his wife are patients. Lucius and Narcissa Malfoy are generous donors to St. Mungo's.

Secrecy Sensor A type of dark-arts-detector that looks like a squiggly gold television aerial. It vibrates when it detects lies and concealment.

Seeker A quidditch position. The seeker's job is to capture the tiny, silver-winged, golden snitch. Capturing the snitch earns one hundred and fifty points and ends the game.

Shield Charm A charm that creates a temporary, invisible barrier that protects against minor curses.

Shrinking Solution An acid-green potion made from a simmered concoction of chopped daisy roots, skinned shrivelfig, sliced dead caterpillars, a dash of leech juice, and the spleen of a rat.

Sickle A silver coin used as wizard money. There are seventeen silver sickles to a gold galleon, and twenty-nine bronze knuts to a silver sickle.

Sinistra, Professor Teacher of Astronomy at Hogwarts.

Skeeter, Rita A disreputable reporter who works for the *Daily Prophet* and has a nasty habit of twisting the truth. Rita is a

heavy-jawed, thick-fingered woman who wears jewelled spectacles and sets her hair in rigid curls. Her brightly painted fingernails are two inches long and she has at least three gold teeth. Skeeter is an unregistered animagus who gets access to confidential information by transforming herself into a black beetle and "bugging" people's private conversations. She uses a quick-quotes quill for her interviews and often carries a crocodile bag.

Skrewt, Blast-ended A magical creature whose fast-growing hatchlings look like slimy, shell-less, six-inch-long lobsters and smell like rotting fish. Adult skrewts are large, armoured creatures that propel themselves forward by expelling sparks from their back ends. Neither immature nor full-grown skrewts have recognizable eyes or heads. Skrewts are vicious creatures that kill one another if they are not properly exercised and that can inflict painful burns and bites. The males have stingers; the females, suckers on their bellies.

Sleekeazy's Hair Potion The hair conditioner that Hermione occasionally uses to tame her bushy hair.

Snape, Severus Professor and head of Slytherin House. Snape is the Potions instructor, but he really wants to be teaching Defence Against the Dark Arts. His classes are held in a cold, creepy dungeon stocked with pickled animals floating in glass jars. Snape has greasy black hair, a hooked nose, sallow skin and cold, empty black eyes. He is a former death eater who renounced Voldemort and turned spy for his former master's enemies—at great risk to himself. He was cleared by the Council of Magical Law and he has the trust of Albus

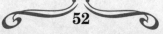

Dumbledore. Snape attended Hogwarts with Harry Potter's father James.

Sneakoscope A glass device that looks like a spinning top and that lights up, spins, and whistles piercingly if it is near someone who is untrustworthy.

Snitch *See* **Golden Snitch**.

Snuffles The alias Sirius Black asks Ron, Hermione and Harry to use when they are talking about him.

Sonorus The magic word used to increase the volume of a person's speaking voice. Ludo Bagman points his wand at his throat and says "*sonorus*" to make himself heard by the crowds at the Quidditch World Cup.

Sorcerer's Stone *See* **Philosopher's Stone**.

Sorting Hat A frayed, patched and very dirty pointed wizard's hat that belonged to Godric Gryffindor, one of the founders of Hogwarts. The sorting hat decides which Hogwarts house each new student will belong to. *See* **Hogwarts School of Witchcraft and Wizardry**.

Spellotape What wizards use for mending rips and tears in books and the like.

S.P.E.W. Society for the Promotion of Elfish Welfare. *See* **Granger, Hermione**.

Sphinx A hybrid creature with the head of a woman and the body of a lion. Passersby must correctly answer her riddle before she allows them to get by her.

Splinch To leave body parts behind during apparition. Half of a splinched body remains in its original location and half is transported to the intended destination. Splinching is corrected by the Accidental Magic Reversal Squad.

Sprout, Professor A squat little witch with flyaway hair under a patched hat. She teaches Herbology, and usually has earth on her clothes and fingernails.

Stoatshead Hill One of two hundred portkey locations arranged to get wizards to the Quidditch World Cup. Located near the village of Ottery St. Catchpole, Stoatshead Hill is the portkey site nearest to the Weasleys'.

Stunner A "peace-keeping officer" employed by the Ministry of Magic. Stunners are also employed to control dragons. Their weapon is the stunning spell.

Stunning Spell A spell used to immobilize people or creatures. The magic word for this spell is *stupefy*.

Stupefy The magic word used in the stunning spell.

Summoning Charm Used to summon hidden objects. The magic word for this charm is *accio*. Harry masters the charm with a lot of help from Hermione, and uses it to summon his flying-broom when he confronts a dragon in the first task of the Triwizard Tournament.

Swedish Short-snout A blue-grey dragon with long, pointed horns.

Switching Spell A simple spell that Professor McGonagall teaches in her Transfiguration class. Neville Longbottom manages to mess up, and transplants his own ears onto a cactus.

Ton-Tongue Toffee A colourfully wrapped candy invented by George and Fred Weasley. The toffee is enchanted with an engorgement charm and eating it can make your tongue grow four feet long. It took the twins six months to perfect the recipe. Dudley Dursley is their first test subject.

Transfiguration Complex, dangerous magic used to turn one thing into something else. Professor McGonagall teaches the Transfiguration class at Hogwarts.

Trelawney, Sybill Professor of Divination at Hogwarts. The professor is a slender, reclusive, bangled and spangled eccentric whose large glasses magnify her eyes to unnatural proportions. She claims that her inner eye allows her to see into the future.

Truth Potion *See* **Veritaserum**.

Triwizard Tournament A friendly competition first established seven hundred years ago to foster ties between wizards and witches of other nations. Europe's three largest schools of wizardry—Beauxbatons, Durmstrang and Hogwarts—take part in the tournament, and each takes a turn at hosting the event. The tournament used to be held every five years. It was suspended more than a century ago due to concerns about the high death rate. Through the efforts of the Departments of International Magical Co-operation and Magical Games and Sports, the tournament is reinstated with new rules in Harry Potter's fourth year at Hogwarts.

The first round of the reinstated tournament is held at Hogwarts, where the goblet of fire selects one seventeen-year-old

champion to represent each competing school. The goblet also selects Harry Potter. The contestants compete in three magical tasks which test their daring, magical prowess, deductive powers, and ability to deal with danger. The winner gets the Triwizard Cup and a thousand galleons in prize money.

The first task of the tournament is scheduled for November 24 and designed to test courage in the face of the unknown. Armed only with their wands, the competitors must grab a golden egg from a nest protected by one of four dragons. Each golden egg holds a clue to the second task. Cheating in the Triwizard Tournament is frowned upon, but the headmasters of Hogwarts' competing schools both give their champions advance information about what the first task will entail. Hagrid levels the playing field by letting Harry in on the secret, and Harry passes the details on to Cedric.

The big day finally arrives. Beauxbatons' champion, Fleur Delacour, faces a common Welsh green, which she subdues by putting it into a trance. Viktor Krum, the Durmstrang champion, gets by his Chinese fireball by using a spell that affects the dragon's eyes. Hogwarts' Cedric Diggory uses transfiguration to distract his Swedish short-snout. Harry captures his egg from a Hungarian horntail by using a summoning charm to get his Firebolt, followed by some very fancy flying. Harry and Viktor are tied for points at the end of the first task.

The second task of the tournament is scheduled for February 24. Cedric returns Harry's favour by telling him how to crack the clue in his egg, which although empty, wails like a banshee

when it is opened. With a bit of help from Moaning Myrtle, Harry discovers that the second challenge is an underwater task that requires him to rescue something important to him within one hour. Dobby the house-elf comes to Harry's aid with gillyweed stolen from Professor Snape. Dobby also tells Harry that the object he must rescue is "his Wheezy"—his best friend, Ron Weasley—whom he must win back from the merpeople.

When Harry eats the gillyweed, he grow gills and flippers that let him swim under water. He gets by several angry grindylows and finds Ron, Hermione, Cho Chang and little Gabrielle Delacour tied to the statue of a huge merperson. Cedric, who has used a bubble-head charm to breathe under water, rescues Cho. Harry helps Viktor, who has transformed into a shark man, to save Hermione. He himself rescues Ron and Gabrielle when Fleur doesn't show up in time. At the end of task two, Harry and Cedric are tied for first place.

The third task, held on June 24, is a maze with twenty-foot-high hedges. The Triwizard Cup is at the centre. The first champion to get by the sphinx and reach the cup gets full points. Harry and Cedric help each other through the maze, and by mutual agreement, touch the cup at the same time. The cup turns out to be a portkey, and they are instantly transported to the graveyard where Voldemort is waiting for Harry. *See* **Goblet of Fire** *and* **Voldemort**.

Unbreakable Charm As the name implies, a charm used to make something unbreakable. Hermione uses this charm on the

glass jar in which she has captured the beetle form of Rita Skeeter, to keep Rita from transforming.

Unforgivable Curse One of the three curses—imperius, cruciatus and avada kedavra—most heavily punished under wizard law. The penalty for using an unforgivable curse is a life sentence in Azkaban.

Unicorn A rare, pure creature whose horns and tail-hair are used in wizards' wands and potions. The unicorn's silver blood has the power to restore life even to someone who is an inch from death. Unicorn foals are pure gold. They turn silver at the age of two, and pure white when they are full-grown, at about the age of seven. They begin to grow horns when they are about four.

Unspeakable A staff position at the Department of Mysteries. Bode and Croaker are unspeakables. No one knows what they really do.

Vector, Professor The witch who teaches Arithmancy at Hogwarts.

Veela *(singular and plural)*. Mesmerizingly beautiful non-human females with white-gold hair and moon-bright skin. Veela serve as mascots for the Bulgarian national quidditch team. They transform into hideous, cruel-beaked birds when they are provoked.

Veritaserum A type of truth potion so powerful that only three drops are required. Veritaserum is clear.

Violet (Vi) A wrinkled old witch who lives in one of the Hogwarts portraits and often comes to visit her friend the Fat Lady.

Voldemort A powerful wizard who goes bad and terrorizes the wizard world, killing all who oppose him and recruiting followers to the dark side. Most wizards fear him so much that they never refer to him by name, but rather, as You-Know-Who or He-Who-Must-Not-Be-Named or the dark lord. Albus Dumbledore is the only wizard Voldemort fears and one of the few who dare to speak his name.

Voldemort kills Harry's parents, James and Lily Potter, who are betrayed by their friend Peter Pettigrew. He tries to kill the one-year-old Harry as well. His murderous green blast leaves Harry with his lightning-shaped scar, but bounces back on Voldemort, turning him into mere shadow and vapour. For many years after the attack, Voldemort can only take on human form when he shares another body. He needs unicorn's blood and the philosopher's stone to regain his former power, but Harry Potter keeps him from getting the needed ingredients. Voldemort attempts another comeback by using his old diary to lure Harry to the chamber of secrets. With the help of the phoenix Fawkes, Harry overcomes the dark lord yet again and destroys the diary with the venomous fang of a basilisk.

Voldemort's third attempt to destroy Harry is almost successful. The unicorn's blood he has drunk has helped him regain a rudimentary human form. He is a hideous, hairless, scaly, red-eyed, reddish-black creature with thin, feeble limbs. The size of a crouched child, he must be carried from place to place.

With the help of Wormtail (Peter Pettigrew), Voldemort feeds on the venom of the serpent Nagini and regains some of his strength. Wormtail brings him Bertha Jorkins, who provides

information that helps the dark lord lay plans for a come-back. He arranges for Harry to take part in the Triwizard Tournament. Barty Crouch Jr. is recruited to assist. He enters Harry's name into the goblet of fire and enchants the Triwizard Cup into a portkey that will bring Harry to Voldemort.

When Harry and Cedric touch the cup, they are transported to the graveyard where Voldemort waits to perform his rebirthing ceremony. Voldemort has not counted on Cedric sharing first place with Harry, and immediately has him killed. The grisly ceremony begins. Wormtail lowers the creature that is Voldemort into a huge cauldron and adds the first ingredient—a bone from the dark lord's father, Tom Riddle Sr. The next ingredient is flesh willingly sacrificed by a servant. It is Wormtail who is chosen for this "honour." He cuts off his right hand and casts it into the cauldron. The final ingredient is the blood of an enemy, and it is Harry's blood that Voldemort demands.

The cauldron simmers and the dark lord is reborn. The Voldemort who emerges is a tall man with blood-red eyes and a flat, snake-like nose. He is thin as a skeleton, with spider-like fingers and slits for pupils and nostrils. Returned to his full strength, he summons his death eaters and challenges Harry to a duel—wand against wand, in wizard fashion. Since Voldemort's wand and Harry's share the same core, priori incantatem (the reverse spell effect) results. The spirits of James and Lily Potter lend Harry the strength he needs to maintain the connection long enough to regain the portkey and make his way back to Hogwarts. For the moment, the

wizard world is safe, but how long can Voldemort's new power be held in check? *See* **Ollivanders**, **Pettigrew**, **Peter** *and* **Potter, James and Lily**.

WWN The Wizarding Wireless Network.

Weasley, Arthur and Molly Ron's parents. Ron's mother, Molly, is a short, plump, kindly woman who conjures wonderful meals and often carries a large clothes brush in her bag. Arthur Weasley is a thin, balding man who wears glasses. Arthur heads the Misuse of Muggle Artifacts Office at the Ministry of Magic and is fascinated by muggles and muggle affairs.

Weasley, Bill The oldest of Ron's red-headed brothers. Bill used to be the Gryffindor head boy. He is now in Egypt, working as a curse-breaker for Gringotts (the wizards' bank).

Weasley, Charlie The second-oldest of Ron's red-headed brothers and an alumnus of Hogwarts. Charlie was captain of Gryffindor's quidditch team. He is now studying dragons in Romania.

Weasley, Fred and George Ron's older brothers, who are identical, red-headed twins. Although the twins are always getting into trouble and constantly scheming up new tricks, they both get really good grades. Harry gives his Triwizard Tournament prize money to Fred and George so that they can start their own joke shop.

Weasley, Ginny The youngest member of the Weasley family and the only girl. Like all of her siblings, Ginny has red hair. She has a crush on Harry Potter. Ginny is a Gryffindor a year behind her brother Ron.

Weasley, Percy One of Ron's red-headed older brothers. Percy accepts a position with the Ministry of Magic when he graduates from Hogwarts. He is hired as the assistant to Bartemius Crouch Sr., who heads the Department of International Magical Co-operation. Percy idolizes his boss, even though Crouch calls him Weatherby instead of Weasley.

Weasley, Ron Harry's best friend. Ron is the sixth child in his family to attend Hogwarts, and like his siblings, he belongs to Gryffindor House. Ron is a tall, thin, gangly, freckle-faced red-head with big hands and feet and a long nose. He never gets anything new, but has to make do with hand-me-downs from his older brothers. Ron is an avid quidditch fan and every inch of his bedroom at home is covered with posters of his favourite team, the Chudley Cannons. His favourite comic books are *The Adventures of Martin Miggs, The Mad Muggle*.

Weasleys' Wizard Wheezes Fake wands, trick candy, joke supplies and other inventions concocted by Fred and George Weasley. The twins' plans to sell their wares at Hogwarts and make some money are dashed when their mother discovers and burns their order forms. *See* **Ton-Tongue Toffee**.

Weatherby The name Percy Weasley is called by his boss, Barty Crouch Sr.

Weird Sisters Popular entertainers whose music is often featured on the Wizarding Wireless Network. Dumbledore engages them to perform at the Hogwarts Yule ball. The sisters are all very hairy. Their stage costume consists of artfully ripped black robes.

Werewolf A creature which endures a painful transformation from human to wolf each month at the full moon. In wolf form, werewolves are dangerous to humans, but not to animals.

Whomping Willow An extremely large and dangerous willow tree that protects itself by hitting out with its branches. The whomping willow was planted in the centre of Hogwarts' quidditch field in James and Lily Potters' time.

Wimple, Gilbert Head of the Committee on Experimental Charms at the Ministry of Magic. Wimple's horns are an occupational hazard.

Winky A tea-towel-garbed, female house-elf who is desperately afraid of heights. Winky belongs to the Crouch family, like her mother and grandmother before her. She is given clothes (that is, dismissed) when she is discovered holding the wand that conjured the dark mark at the Quidditch World Cup. She makes her way to Hogwarts with her friend Dobby, but her freedom weighs heavily on her and she refuses to accept pay for her work. *See* **House-elf**.

Wit-sharpening Potion One of the potions Hoggarts students learn to make in their fourth-year Potions class. Its ingredients include ginger roots, armadillo bile and powdered scarab beetles.

Witch Weekly A popular magazine which runs an unflattering piece that Rita Skeeter writes about Hermione.

Wizarding Wireless Network (WWN) The wizards' radio station, which often features popular musical groups like the Weird Sisters.

Wood, Oliver Former captain and keeper for the Gryffindor quidditch team. Oliver has just graduated from Hogwarts and now plays quidditch with the Puddlemere United reserve team.

Wormtail Peter Pettigrew's nickname when he was a student at Hogwarts. *See* **Animagus**; **Lupin, Remus**; **Pettigrew, Peter** *and* **Voldemort**.

Wronski Feint A quidditch manoeuvre in which the seeker pretends to dive for the snitch, luring his opponent to follow after. The instigator of the manoeuvre pulls up at the last possible moment, often causing the seeker who is in pursuit to crash into the ground. Viktor Krum is a master of the Wronski Feint.

You-Know-Who *See* **Voldemort**.

Yule Ball A traditional part of the Triwizard Tournament. The ball is intended to promote socialization between the competing schools. Dress robes are mandatory. Only students in their fourth, fifth, sixth or seventh years may attend although they may invite younger students to be their escorts if they so wish.